best
easy
day hikes
Glacier and
Waterton Lakes

Erik Molvar

FALCON®

HELENA, MONTANA

© 1998 by Falcon® Publishing Inc. Helena, Montana
Printed in Canada.

3   4   5   6   7   8   9   10   TP   05   04   03   02   01   00

Cataloging-in-Publication Data is on record at the Library of Congress.

CAUTION

Outdoor recreational activities are by their very nature potentially hazardous. All participants in such activities must assume responsibility for their own actions and safety. The information contained in this guidebook cannot replace sound judgment and good decision-making skills, which help reduce risk exposure, nor does the scope of this book allow for disclosure of all the potential hazards and risks involved in such activities.

Learn as much as possible about the outdoor recreational activities in which you participate, prepare for the unexpected, and be cautious. The reward will be a safer and more enjoyable experience.

 Text pages printed on recycled paper.

Contents

Acknowledgments

Thanks to Jack Potter, Randall Schwanke, and Locke Marshall for providing information and reviewing this material. The introductory material is largely the work of Bill Schneider, while Ron Adkison wrote most of the "Hiking with Kids" section. Special thanks to my fiancée, Melanie Davidson, for providing good company during the field research.

Legend

Interstate	
U.S. Highway	
State or County Road	
Interstate Highway	
Paved Road	
Unpaved Road, Graded	
Unpaved Road, Poor	
Trailhead	
Main Trail	
Secondary Trail	
Trailless Route	
River/Creek, Perennial	
Rapids	
Drainage, Intermittent Creek	
Spring	
Forest/Wilderness/ Park Boundary	
State Boundary	

Picnic Area

Campground

Bridge

Mine Site

City Grid

Cabins/Buildings

Ranger Station

Elevation
X
9,782 ft.

Mountain/Peak

Falls, Pouroff

Pass/Saddle

Gate

Glacier

Map Orientation
N

Scale
0   30   60
Miles

IDAHO

MONTANA

Glacier and Waterton Lakes National Parks

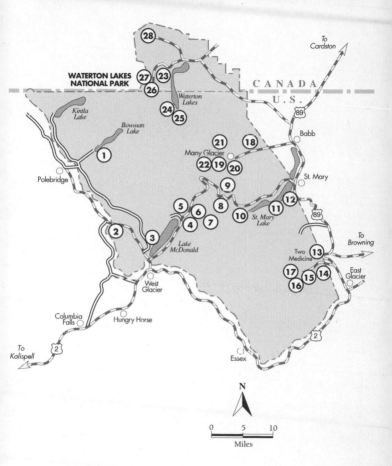

Introduction

What's a "best easy" hike?

Our national parks and forests serve as windows to the natural world, reservoirs of natural beauty and grandeur, and wellsprings of inspiration. As such, they are magnets to people who seek to reestablish their ties with nature, learn more about the world in which we live, or simply find a quiet escape from the hustle and bustle of modern society. Glacier National Park and its Canadian neighbor, Waterton, feature mountain fastnesses clad in glaciers, azure lakes, and sparkling waterfalls, inviting the visitor to step into the natural world.

Anyone who travels widely in these areas will soon notice that park visitors fall into two distinct categories—those who want to immerse themselves in wilderness backcountry for several days at a time, and those who have only a day or two and would like a choice sampling of the area's special features. This book is for the second group.

I gathered materials for this guide as I researched the much larger and more comprehensive *Hiking Glacier and Waterton Lakes National Parks.* That book covers every trail in both parks, including those which are neither best nor easy. *Best Easy Day Hikes Glacier and Waterton Lakes* includes only short, less strenuous hikes that showcase the best features of the region.

These hikes vary in length, but most are short. Most lack big hills, and the few long grades that appear in this book can be tackled in a leisurely fashion. All hikes are on easy-to-follow trails with no off-trail route-finding challenges. Trailhead access is easy for all hikes, and you can reach any of these trailheads with a low-clearance passenger car.

Some of the hikes in this book might not seem easy to some, but they will be easy for others. To help you decide what trails are right for you, I've ranked the hikes from easiest to hardest in the following pages. Please keep in mind that long does not always equal difficult. Other factors, such as elevation gain and trail conditions, have to be considered.

I hope you thoroughly enjoy your "best easy" hiking through the natural wonders of Glacier and Waterton Lakes national parks.

—Erik Molvar

Ranking the Hikes

The following list ranks the hikes in this book from easiest to most difficult:

Easiest

Trail of the Cedars
Swiftcurrent Nature Trail
Running Eagle Falls
Blakiston Falls
Rainbow Falls
Cameron Lake
Sun Point Nature Trail
Kootenai Lakes
Huckleberry Mountain Nature Trail
Beaver Pond Trail
Bullhead Lake
Johns Lake Loop
McDonald Creek
Grinnell Lake
McDonald Lake Trail
Bowman Lake
Lower Bertha Falls
St. Mary and Virginia Falls
Upper Two Medicine Lake
Avalanche Lake
Appistoki Falls
Hidden Lake
Two Medicine Lake
Aster Park
Lineham Falls
Haystack Butte
Iceberg Lake

Most Difficult   Apikuni Falls

Zero Impact

Traveling in a national park such as Glacier is like visiting a famous museum. You obviously don't want to leave your mark on an art treasure. If everybody who visited the museum left one tiny mark, the piece of art would be destroyed—and what would a big building full of trashed art be worth? The same goes for pristine wilderness such as that found in the Northern Rockies. If we all left just one little mark on the landscape, the wilderness would soon be despoiled.

A wilderness can accommodate plenty of human use as long as everybody treats it with respect. But a few thoughtless or uninformed visitors can ruin it for everyone who follows. And the need for good manners applies to all wilderness visitors, not just backpackers. Day hikers should also adhere strictly to "zero impact" principles. We all must pass through the landscape respectfully, leaving no clues that we have gone before.

Three FalconGuide Principles of Zero Impact
- *Leave with everything you brought with you.*
- *Leave no sign of your visit.*
- *Leave the landscape as you found it.*

Most of us know better than to litter, in or out of the wilderness. Even the tiniest scrap of paper left along the trail or at a campsite detracts from the landscape's pristine character. This means that you should pack out everything, even biodegradable items such as orange peels, which can take years to decompose. It's also a good idea to pick up any trash that less considerate hikers have left behind.

To avoid damaging the trailside soil and plants, stay on the main path. Avoid cutting switchbacks and venturing onto fragile vegetation. When taking a rest stop, select a durable surface like a bare log, rock, or sandy beach. Don't pick up "souvenirs," such as rocks, antlers, feathers, or wildflowers. The next person wants to discover them, too, and taking such souvenirs violates park regulations.

Avoid making loud noises that disturb the silence others may be enjoying. Remember, sound travels easily in the outdoors. Be courteous. When nature calls, use established outhouse facilities whenever possible. If these are unavailable, bury human waste 6 to 8 inches deep and pack out used toilet paper. This is a good reason to carry a lightweight trowel. Keep wastes at least 300 feet away from any surface water or boggy spots.

Finally, and perhaps most importantly, strictly follow the pack-it-in/pack-it-out rule. If you carry something into the wilderness, consume it completely or carry it out with you. Zero impact—put your ear to the ground in the wilderness and listen carefully. The thousands of people coming behind you are thanking you for your courtesy and good sense.

Hiking With Kids

Hiking with children can be one of the most rewarding and memorable experiences a family can undertake. Hiking offers a tremendous learning opportunity, giving children confidence and a growing awareness of the world around them. Kids can enrich the hiking experiences of their parents as well, since they often find beauty in small details that adults overlook.

Choose a destination that is accessible to your kids, and set your goals with your youngest child's abilities in mind. If you are carrying a young child in a kid-carrier backpack, you may be able to travel farther than you could if that child were walking. Young children can surprise you with their ability to travel long distances, if parents are willing to shoulder some of the extra load.

As a general rule, children two to four years old can be expected to walk up to 2 miles per day, taking rest stops every ten to fifteen minutes. Children five to seven years of age can usually hike up to 4 miles per day, and should rest every thirty to forty-five minutes. Once children reach eight or nine years of age, they can be expected to cover up to 7 miles a day.

Start with short trips so the kids can get accustomed to hiking uneven trails. Children tire quickly and are easily distracted, so don't be surprised if you don't make it to your destination. Stay flexible and consider alternate turnaround points en route to your goal. Point out special sights, sounds, and smells along the way to help your children enjoy the trip and learn about what they see. If you make the hike fun, keeping the kids interested, they will keep going.

Careful planning with an emphasis on safety will help make your trip an enjoyable one. Allow older children to carry their own packs, and perhaps bring a favorite toy or book along. These things, along with some equipment kids can carry, help develop a sense of responsibility and teach young hikers the advantages of packing light. Children over age four can carry a day pack, but parents should be prepared to carry the pack for a tired child. Limit the weight of an older child's pack to 20 percent of the child's body weight. Parents may have to carry some of the child's gear.

Young skin is very sensitive to the sun and to insect bites. Apply sunscreen to your kids before and during the trip. Carry a good insect repellant, preferably a natural product, and apply it as necessary. Also consider carrying a product that takes the itch out of insect bites. A hat helps keep bright sun out of sensitive young eyes. Rain gear is always an important consideration in the mountains, since storms and cold weather tend to move in unexpectedly. Kids seem to have less tolerance to cold than adults, so bring ample warm clothing. If your hike will take you to the edge of a river or lake, careful supervision of your kids is a must. Consider bringing a life vest for your child.

Parents should be aware that both grizzly bears and mountain lions range throughout the park. Make sure that your group stays together, and do not let children run ahead.

Among your important considerations when hiking with children should be the wilderness experience of other hikers. Kids are naturally inclined to run around, chase animals, collect flowers and rocks, and shatter the silence with their screams. These behaviors may be fine in town, but they are inappropriate in a wilderness setting. Always be aware that many visitors who seek out the wild country of Glacier do so to find tranquillity and solitude. Supervise your children so that their actions do not impose on others. Finally, since children learn by example, day hiking offers an excellent opportunity to instruct children in the arts of treading lightly and reducing their impacts on the landscape.

Lake McDonald and The North Fork Country

OVERVIEW

Lake McDonald, near the west entrance of Glacier National Park, is the largest body of water in the park. It is 10 miles long and has a maximum depth of 472 feet. The lakebed was carved out by a huge glacier that filled the entire valley, leaving a characteristic U-shaped basin. Lake McDonald was once fair fishing for native cutthroat trout, but ever since the introduction of lake trout wiped out the cutthroat population, the lake has offered very poor fishing. At the lake's foot lie the low foothills of the Apgar Range and the Belton Hills, while snowcapped peaks along the Continental Divide loom to the east of the lake's head. The country is characterized by low, east-west ridges rising to rugged peaks. Dense forests cover the entire area, grading from cedars, birches, and larches at lower elevations to Douglas-firs and lodgepole pines higher up.

The North Fork of the Flathead River occupies a forested valley bounded on the west by the Whitefish Range and on the east by the craggy Livingston Range. The climate here reflects a maritime influence, with storm fronts pushing in from the Pacific Ocean. As a result, the North Fork country gets quite a bit of precipitation over the course of a year, most of which falls in wintertime as snow.

Lodgepole pines dominate the vegetation of the valley floor, dependent on periodic fires to maintain their competitive edge over more shade-tolerant species. The serotinous cones of lodgepoles are covered with resin that melts and allows the cone to release seeds only in the presence of heat provided by forest fires. The seeds then fall on fertile soil in openings created by the fire, where they germinate and thrive in direct sunlight. The most recent blaze in the park was the Red Bench Fire of 1988, which burned much of the North Fork valley.

Hikes around Lake McDonald and the North Fork tend to pass through heavy forest, with limited opportunities for sweeping views. Burns and lakes provide occasional vistas. The forest itself abounds with wild berries in late summer. Lakes and streams typically harbor native west-slope cutthroat trout, though rainbow trout were introduced in some areas. In general, the lakes provide much better fishing than the streams, which are so pure that they contain few nutrients to sustain a productive food web. Know the park fishing regulations and check for closures and catch limits before you set out.

Wildlife in this part of Glacier reflects the boreal nature of the region, with elk and white-tailed deer being plentiful. Taiga species, such as lynx and fisher, are occasionally seen in thick stands of lodgepole pine at lower elevations. The North Fork country is home to several active wolf packs, which colonized the park naturally from Canada. Hikers who see tracks or hear the howl of these endangered predators can consider themselves truly fortunate. Birders will

Lake McDonald and the North Fork Country

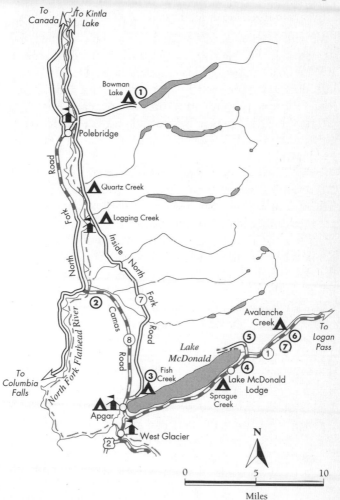

find the large glacial lakes of this area good places to see ospreys, bald eagles, and common loons.

West Glacier, Montana, is the western gateway to the park and serves as trailhead and rafting hub for the park's western side. Vendors offer a wide variety of tourist services at West Glacier, Apgar Village, and Lake McDonald Lodge, including guided horse trips, gas, restaurants, and lodging. Major car campgrounds are located at Apgar and Avalanche Creek; these tend to be crowded and noisy. A quieter tents-only campground is located on Sprague Creek near Lake McDonald Lodge.

The North Fork valley can be accessed via the Inside North Fork Road (Glacier Route 7), a narrow gravel road that runs along the river inside the park boundary. There are auto campgrounds at Quartz and Logging creeks along the way, as well as campgrounds at the foot of Bowman and Kintla lakes. An alternate route into the North Fork area is the Polebridge Road, which can be accessed from the terminus of the Camas Road or from the town of Columbia Falls, Montana, and runs 16 miles north to the settlement of Polebridge. This road, heavily traveled by logging trucks, is frequently in rough condition. Polebridge is an authentic frontier community, serving a handful of homesteads and ranches on the west bank of the river. This "town" boasts a mercantile store selling gas and groceries and the Northern Lights Saloon, which serves meals and libations to weary travelers in an atmosphere of down-home hospitality. Just north of this quaint community, a new two-lane bridge crosses the river to link up with Glacier Route 7.

1
BOWMAN LAKE

Type of hike: Out-and-back.
Total distance: Up to 14 miles (round trip).
Time required: 1 to 9 hours, depending on length of hike.
Elevation change: Minimal.
Finding the trailhead: Follow Glacier Route 7 north to its junction with the Bowman Lake Road, just north of Polebridge. Take the Bowman Lake Rd. (a narrow but graded gravel road) to its terminus at Bowman Campground. The trail departs from the northeast corner of the campground, near the lakeshore.

Key points:
0.0   Trail sign. Trail follows shore of Bowman Lake.
0.7   Junction with Numa Lookout trail. Stay right.
7.1   Campground at head of Bowman Lake.

The hike: This trail follows the northwestern shore of Bowman Lake for 7 miles of gentle up-and-down hiking. It may be used as a backpack route in itself, or as a day hike of any length along the lakeshore. The trail winds past Bowman Lake before ascending a U-shaped valley carved by a glacier between rugged peaks. Views across the lake include the glacier-carved summits of Square Peak, Rainbow Peak, and Mount Carter. The lake is prime osprey and bald eagle habitat, and its waters frequently are closed to boating, fishing,

Bowman Lake

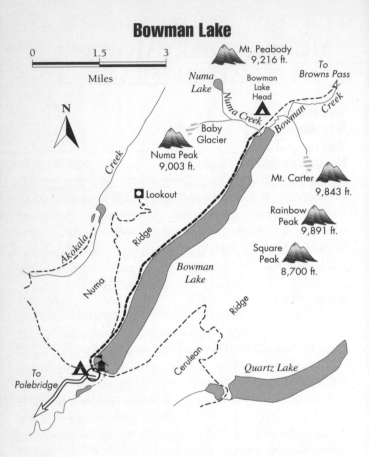

and hiking above the upper campground to protect active eagle nests. Loons frequently are sighted on the lake's surface. The backcountry campsite near the head of the lake is popular with hikers and boaters alike.

2
HUCKLEBERRY MOUNTAIN NATURE TRAIL

Type of hike: Loop.
Total distance: 0.9 mile.
Time required: 20 to 45 minutes.
Elevation change: 120-foot gain.
Finding the trailhead: The trail leaves from a parking area on the south side of the Camas Road, 0.2 mile east of the Camas Entrance Station.

The hike: This self-guiding loop trail visits the thirty-year-old burn at the foot of Huckleberry Mountain. A pamphlet available at the trailhead sheds light on the forest regeneration that follows a fire.

The trail begins on benches clad in lodgepole pine. Gaps between the young conifers are occupied by swards of tall grass, providing forage for herbivores as diverse as mice and elk. Watch for the tall, bright fuchsia spikes of the flower known as fireweed. This opportunistic plant relies on wind-borne seeds to colonize the charred soil of recent burns. It thrives in sunlight and on the abundant nutrients available in the wake of a blaze. A few spikes of this flower remain here in the open spots among the pines.

After dropping into a draw, the path climbs onto the lower slopes of Huckleberry Mountain, where skeletal snags of ancient larches tower overhead. As the path turns west

Huckleberry Mountain Nature Trail

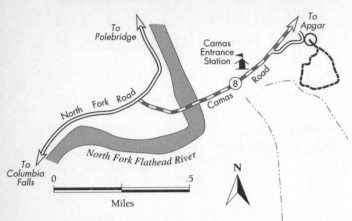

and starts to descend, watch for a sparse growth of surviving larches rising above the regenerating lodgepoles. Both larch and lodgepole pine are considered fire-adapted species, but they have contrasting adaptations to fire. Larch has a thick and corky bark of puzzle-piece construction. As it burns, this bark flakes away from the trunk of the tree, preventing the living inner bark or cambium from being scorched. Adult larches are often the only trees to survive a blaze, and these survivors have a head start in reseeding the burn. In contrast, lodgepole pine has no protection against the flames. Adult lodgepoles may die in the flames, but they have special serotinous cones sealed with pitch. The fire's heat melts away the pitch, and the cones release their seeds over the burned soil. Neither larch nor lodgepole pine does well in the shade—their seedlings cannot survive without direct sunlight. If the forest remains unburned for several centuries, these trees inexorably will be replaced by shade-tolerant species, such as Engelmann spruce.

After a vigorous climb onto the mountainside, the trail dips to the edge of an old-growth stand of spruce that survived the fire. It then wanders through a meadow of rank grasses where herbivores come to graze during twilight hours.

3
McDONALD LAKE TRAIL

Type of hike: Shuttle.
Total distance: 6.6 miles.
Time required: 3 to 5 hours.
Elevation change: 160-foot gain and loss.
Finding the trailhead: From Apgar, follow the Camas Road north for 0.8 mile and turn right at the sign for Fish Creek Campground. Follow the Inside North Fork Road past the campground ranger station. As the road turns to gravel, look for a road information sign with a parking area a short distance beyond it on the left-hand side. Park here; the hike begins on the opposite side of the road.

Key points:
0.0   Trailhead on North Fork Road.
0.1   Trail crosses Fern Creek.
0.4   Junction with trail from Fish Creek Campground. Bear left.
0.5   Junction with Rocky Point spur trail (0.3 mile).
4.6   Spur trail descends to McDonald Lake Camp (0.2 mile).
6.6   Trail reaches end of North Shore Road.

The hike: This relatively obscure and lightly traveled trail follows the roadless northwestern shore of Lake McDonald. The trail stays mostly within heavy forest, but at several

McDonald Lake Trail

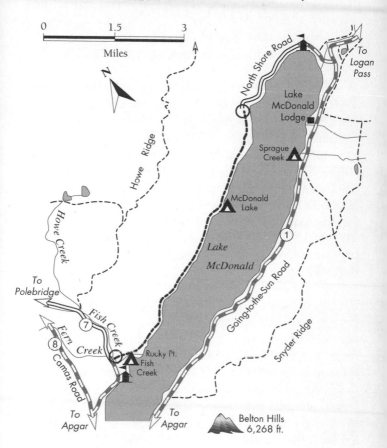

0   1.5   3
Miles

N

North Shore Road

To Logan Pass

Lake McDonald Lodge

Sprague Creek

Howe Ridge

McDonald Lake

Howe Creek

Lake McDonald

1

To Polebridge

Howe Creek

Fish Creek

Going-to-the-Sun Road

Snyder Ridge

7

Fern Creek

8

Camas Road

Rocky Pt.
Fish Creek

To Apgar

To Apgar

Belton Hills
6,268 ft.

isolated points it visits the lakeshore for outstanding views of the surrounding country. Hikers seeking a shorter trip can start at the south end and visit Rocky Point (1.6 miles, round-trip), or start from the northern end of the trail and hike to the Lake McDonald backcountry camp (4.4 miles, round-trip).

After crossing a bridge over Fern Creek, the trail runs through a young forest of lodgepole pine underlain by bear grass. This forest community is typical of post-fire coniferous forests in northwestern Montana. The path soon meets a broad trail that begins in the Fish Creek Campground. Follow this wide avenue northeast along the lakeshore to reach a junction with the side trail that runs to a headland known as Rocky Point. This side trip is well worth the effort and ends on an outcrop with superb views up Lake McDonald. The sharp crags above the lake's head are, from left to right, Mount Brown, the Little Matterhorn, Edwards Peak, Gunsight Mountain, and Mount Jackson.

Meanwhile, the Lake McDonald trail makes a stiff climb inland, entering the Halfmoon Burn of 1929. Young trees grow densely here, competing to become dominant members of the forest overstory. The path next emerges from the forest at a pebble beach at mile 1.8; here hikers can see Mount Cannon along with the summits mentioned earlier. The trail then enters a mature, unburned forest where conifers rise several hundred feet above a sparse and shady understory. Western redcedar and hemlock are the most abundant trees, but larch, black cottonwood, and white pine also grow here.

The trail runs close to the shoreline now, revealing glimpses of turquoise water through the foliage.

At mile 4.6, a spur trail descends to the Lake McDonald backcountry camp, which is situated on a timbered point. One can look both up and down Lake McDonald from the gravel beach of this point, with views all the way up the McDonald Creek valley to the Garden Wall. Mounts Stanton and Vaught can now be seen above the north side of the lake.

The main trail continues through deep forest, where many trees have attained old-growth dimensions. The trail swings inland shortly before joining an old dirt road, which it follows to reach the eastern trailhead at the end of the North Shore Road.

4
JOHNS LAKE LOOP

Type of hike: Loop or shuttle.
Total distance: 2.4 miles.
Time required: 1 to 2 hours.
Elevation change: 100-foot gain and loss.
Finding the trailhead: Follow Going-to-the-Sun Road northeast from Lake McDonald Lodge for 1.5 miles. Park at the Johns Lake Trailhead on the right side of the road, just before the junction with the North Shore Road.

Key points:
0.0   Johns Lake Trailhead.
0.2   Trail joins McDonald horse trail. Turn left.
0.7   Johns Lake trail splits away from horse loop. Turn right.
0.9   Johns Lake. Junction with Avalanche Creek Trail. Turn left.
1.1   Trail crosses Going-to-the-Sun Road. Bear right on road to link with Sacred Dancing Cascade access ramp.
1.2   Bridge over McDonald Creek.
1.3   Junction with McDonald Creek Trail. Turn left, then left again onto primitive streambank trail (marked "no horses").
1.5   McDonald Falls.
2.1   Trail emerges on North Shore Road. Turn left to complete loop.
2.4   Johns Lake Trailhead.

Johns Lake Loop

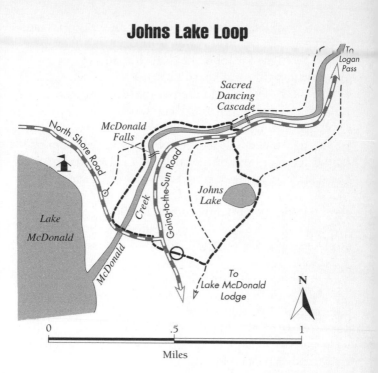

The hike: This popular loop runs through the forest above the head of Lake McDonald, visiting a woodland lake as well as Sacred Dancing Cascade and McDonald Falls along McDonald Creek. Parts of the trail receive heavy horse use from trail rides that originate at Lake McDonald Lodge.

The hike begins with a moderate climb into the cedar-hemlock forest south of Going-to-the-Sun Road. Turn left at the first junction as the trail rises into an old burn populated by Douglas-fir and lodgepole pine. Beargrass and huckleberry thrive in the sunny understory found here. Follow the signs for Johns Lake as the path returns to the closed-canopy forest. The path reaches Johns Lake 0.2 mile later. This shallow pool in the woodlands reflects the summits of mounts Stanton and Vaught.

A connecting trail runs northward from the lakeshore toward Avalanche Lake; avoid it in favor of the wider path bound for Going-to-the-Sun Road. This trail descends through the deep shade of western hemlocks, and a carpet of moss covers the forest floor. Upon reaching the road, cross the crosswalk and turn right (north) to reach the paved pathway that descends to Sacred Dancing Cascade. Cross McDonald Creek on the bridge just below a stairstep waterfall.

On the far bank, turn left (south) and choose the primitive path with the "no horses" sign. This path follows the rims of low cliffs that guard McDonald Creek, with fine views of riffled whitewater and turquoise pools. The path soon reaches McDonald Falls, and a spur track runs to the lip where water plunges as a thundering cataract. The trail then wanders through a bottomland hemlock forest to reach the North Shore Road. Shuttle hikers should turn right on this road to reach the McDonald Creek trailhead; loop hikers turn left, crossing the road bridge then following a horse trail back to the Johns Lake Trailhead. During wet weather, stick to the road to avoid horse-churned mud.

5
McDONALD CREEK

Type of hike: Out-and-back.
Total distance: A 6.8-mile round trip.
Time required: 3 to 5 hours.
Elevation change: 200-foot gain.
Finding the trailhead: From Lake McDonald Lodge, follow Going-to-the-Sun Road northeast for several miles to the junction with the North Shore Road. Turn left, crossing the bridge over McDonald Creek to reach the marked trailhead on the right side of the road.

Key points:
0.0   North Shore Road.
0.9   Bridge over McDonald Creek. Stay on north bank of creek.
2.2   Horse turnaround point.
3.4   Trail ends at edge of gorge.

The hike: This short hike follows a fragment of the old packer's trail that ran up the McDonald Creek valley before Going-to-the-Sun Road was built. Here McDonald Creek is guarded by the low walls of a distinctive little gorge, its aquamarine waters flow down as rushing waterfalls and quiet runs. Part of the trail is used for trail rides originating at Lake McDonald Lodge, so be prepared to meet horses along

McDonald Creek and Avalanche Lake

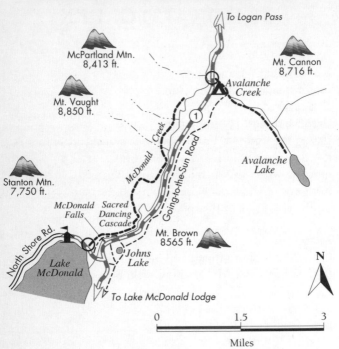

To Logan Pass

McPartland Mtn.
8,413 ft.

Mt. Cannon
8,716 ft.

Avalanche
Creek

Mt. Vaught
8,850 ft.

McDonald Creek

Going-to-the-Sun Road

Avalanche
Lake

Stanton Mtn.
7,750 ft.

McDonald
Falls

Sacred
Dancing
Cascade

Mt. Brown
8565 ft.

North Shore Rd.

Johns
Lake

Lake
McDonald

To Lake McDonald Lodge

N

0   1.5   3

Miles

the way. The hike is particularly striking in the silence of early winter, when massive icicles hang from the walls of the gorge.

The trail begins by wandering northwest through a mixed woodland of hemlock, larch, and Douglas-fir occupying the bottomlands along McDonald Creek. After a short journey, the path approaches the stream, with its turquoise waters swirling down between slanted slabs of stone. To view the roaring cataract of McDonald Falls, take a short side trip down the stream bank on an unofficial trail marked with a "no horses" sign. The main path now runs northeast along the rim of a small gorge. The crenelated facade of Mount Brown looms across the valley, a constant presence along this portion of the route. The path soon reaches the sturdy bridge over Sacred Dancing Cascade, and just upstream the water descends gracefully across a lengthy series of tiny stairsteps.

The wider path leads across the stream to a parking area and beyond to Johns Lake; the McDonald Creek Trail is the narrow gravel pathway that continues upstream along the north bank of the creek. After passing a small waterfall, the trail turns inland to enter the silent hallways of climax coniferous forest. Where it next emerges, streamside, the waters glide placidly through cedar bottoms. The lofty edifice of Mount Cannon rises ahead, and soon Mount Vaught and Heavens Peak appear on the north side of the valley. Watch for moose as well as beaver, which have dammed some of the slow moving backwaters in this area.

The path then wanders inland, passing through a deep forest of hemlock. At mile 2.2, the horse tours turn around at a wide spot in the timber. A more primitive path continues onward, becoming overgrown with low brush for a short stretch. It soon crosses a gravelly wash where floodwaters from the slopes of Mount Vaught have buried the tree trunks in rocky debris. On the far side of the streamcourse, the path improves for a long sojourn through hemlock forest. Travelers are rewarded as the trail emerges beside the rocky upper gorge of McDonald Creek. Here, waters churn over violent waterfalls, and the imposing summit of Mount Cannon rises regally above the stream. Watch your step; there are no guardrails here to prevent a tumble into the churning whitewater. The path ends suddenly atop the bedrock with views of a particularly impressive falls.

6
TRAIL OF THE CEDARS

Type of hike: Loop.
Total distance: 0.7 mile.
Time required: 20 to 60 minutes.
Elevation change: Minimal.
Finding the trailhead: Trail of the Cedars Trailhead, across from Avalanche Picnic Area on Going-to-the-Sun Road.

Key points:
0.0   Trail of the Cedars Trailhead. Follow the boardwalk.
0.4   Bridge below Avalanche Gorge. Follow paved trail down south bank of stream.
0.7   Old Avalanche Creek Campground entrance on Going-to-the-Sun Road.

The hike: This self-guiding nature trail forms a loop through old-growth forest in the bottoms of Avalanche Creek. Avalanche Gorge lies at the apex of the loop, with swirling waters and sculpted argillite walls. The northern leg of the trail follows a boardwalk, while the southern leg is paved, with benches along the way so hikers can stop and enjoy the grandeur of the forest. The entire loop is wheelchair accessible.

From the trailhead, follow the boardwalk that runs through the forest north of Avalanche Creek. The

Trail of the Cedars

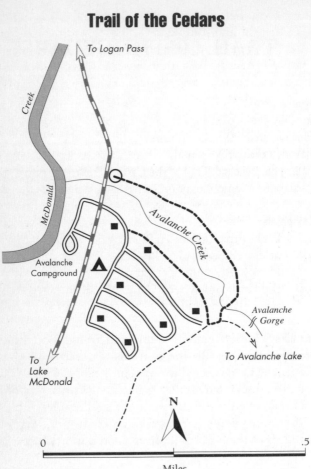

To Logan Pass

Creek

McDonald

Avalanche Creek

Avalanche Campground

To Lake McDonald

Avalanche Gorge

To Avalanche Lake

N

0   .5

Miles

old-growth that rises from these damp and fertile bottoms has remained undisturbed for centuries, and the trees have grown tall and stout in the absence of fire and avalanche. The oldest trees are western redcedar and black cottonwood, species more commonly found along coastal rivers of the Pacific Northwest. Ferns and devil's club occupy the understory. Most of the younger trees are western hemlock, which can be identified by its drooping treetop leader. It is the most shade-tolerant of Glacier's conifers, and its seedlings can thrive beneath a closed-canopy forest where those of other species cannot.

Note the diversity of tree sizes and ages. As the oldest trees succumb to disease and fall to the forest floor, they create sunny gaps in the canopy so that light can reach the ground and allow new seedlings to take root. Over the span of centuries, this gradual replacement of the stand results in a broad diversity of tree heights, forming a multilayered canopy that offers a multitude of ecological niches for forest creatures with specialized diets and food-gathering techniques—such forest dwellers as birds, voles, and squirrels. It is this diversity of plant and animal life that makes old-growth forest so valuable from an ecological standpoint.

As it makes its way through the forest, the boardwalk passes a mossy outcrop of stone. Water seeps constantly from the fissures in this rock, and in winter great stalactites of ice form here. The path then crosses a bridge at the mouth of Avalanche Gorge, where water has carved a deep and whorled channel into the argillite. Moss grows thick at the edges of the gorge, thriving in the constant mist provided by a waterfall just upstream. Watch for a small, gray bird known as the water ouzel, which nests behind waterfalls and makes frequent dives into the current in a quest for aquatic insects.

On the far bank of the creek, a paved path leads westward, following Avalanche Creek as it passes through an abandoned loop of the Avalanche Creek Campground. Note the differences in the forest understory here compared to that of the far bank. It will take centuries for the forest to recover from the clearing of underbrush and the compacting of soil that once took place here. Follow the paved path back to Going-to-the-Sun Road, then turn right (north) to return to your vehicle.

7
AVALANCHE LAKE

see map on page 26

Type of hike: Out-and-back.
Total distance: 4.6 miles (round trip) to foot of lake.
Time required: 2 to 4 hours.
Elevation change: 505-foot gain.
Finding the trailhead: Trail of the Cedars trailhead, across from Avalanche Picnic Area on Going-to-the-Sun Road.

Key points:
0.0   Trail of the Cedars boardwalk.
0.3   Trail leaves boardwalk and crosses Avalanche Creek.
       Junction with Avalanche Creek Trail. Turn left.
2.3   Foot of Avalanche Lake.
3.1   Head of Avalanche Lake.

The hike: The Avalanche Lake Trail is one of the most popular hikes in Glacier, due to its gentle grade and spectacular destination. Hikers seeking solitude should go elsewhere, since throngs of bearbell-bedecked tourists are a given at the height of the season.

The hike begins on the Trail of the Cedars (Hike 6), a boardwalk that winds between boles of huge cedars and cottonwoods to Avalanche Gorge. The gorge was formed by the force of a stream cutting down through argillite beds, creating fantastic bowls and chutes in the rock. The spray from small waterfalls provides the moisture needed to sustain the profusion of mosses that drape the rocks surrounding the gorge. Water ouzels fly along the watercourse, occasionally diving into the churning water, emerging unharmed to execute "pushups" on the rocks along the stream.

The Avalanche Lake Trail follows the west rim of the gorge through stands of western hemlock, identified by its drooping topmost leader. This tree is limited to areas of high rainfall. The trail winds upward through the forest, following the course of Avalanche Creek. Across the valley to the northeast, the Hidden Creek valley joins the valley of Avalanche Creek. The trail continues upward through sparse timber and dense underbrush until it reaches the foot of the lake.

Avalanche Lake is rimmed by steep cliffs on three sides. Bearhat Mountain forms the east wall of the valley, while the west wall is formed by Mount Brown. To the south, at the head of the valley, numerous waterfalls cascade downward from the hanging cirque formed by Sperry Glacier, which cannot be seen from the lake.

Logan Pass and
The St. Mary Valley

OVERVIEW

Logan Pass is one of the most popular destinations in Glacier National Park. High above the timberline at 6,646 feet, it sits in a landscape of vast alpine meadows dotted with bulb-shaped blossoms of bear grass as well as other wildflowers. Stark crags rise all around, and mountain goats are often spotted on the grassy swards below the cliffs. The visitor center at Logan Pass has limited parking, and during the height of summer visitors should come early or plan to take the shuttle.

The St. Mary River drainage is bisected by the Going-to-the-Sun Road, which provides easy access to a well-developed trail system. The most dominant feature of the area is St. Mary Lake itself, reflecting stunning vistas of the surrounding mountains. The front ranges are formed of Grinnell argillite, which imparts a characteristic reddish tint to the peaks. The rainshadow formed by the Continental Divide explains the lack of snow on the eastern peaks during July and August. The peaks along the backbone of the divide have snowfields that linger year-round. A few small glaciers remain in the higher cirques, harking back to the time when the entire park was buried in ice.

Logan Pass and the St. Mary Valley

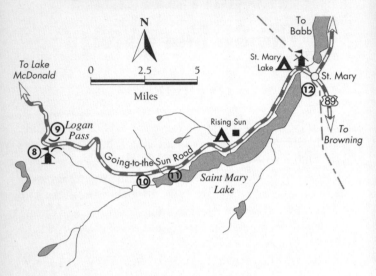

The grassy flats around Rising Sun provide important winter range for elk, and in autumn the bugling of bulls echoes from the valley walls. The valley is dominated by lodgepole pines at its lower elevations, with a few stands of aspen in areas of waterlogged soil. Higher up, spruce and subalpine fir are interspersed with beargrass and other wildflowers. Dry, south-facing slopes are covered with the drought-resistant grasses that dominate the high plains to the east.

The town of St. Mary provides visitor facilities, including a first-rate lodge that occasionally serves lake whitefish, a delicacy caught in nearby lakes. A visitor center just inside the park boundary gives out information and backcountry permits. Half a mile beyond the entrance station is the St. Mary auto campground. Rising Sun includes a motel and camp store, as well as a park-run auto campground. A commercial boat runs tours from Rising Sun, featuring scenic and interpretive loop cruises on St. Mary Lake.

8
HIDDEN LAKE

Type of hike: Out-and-back.
Total distance: 3 miles, round-trip to overlook; 6 miles, round-trip to lake.
Time required: 1.5 to 2.5 hours to overlook; 3 to 5 hours to lake.
Elevation change: 550-foot gain, 670-foot loss.
Finding the trailhead: Trail begins immediately behind Logan Pass Visitor Center.

Key points:
0.0   Trail sign behind Logan Pass Visitor Center.
1.4   Hidden Lake Pass.
1.5   Hidden Lake overlook. Trail descends fairly steeply to Hidden Lake.
3.0   Hidden Lake.

The hike: The trail to Hidden Lake provides some of the quickest access to high alpine country in Glacier National Park. It starts as a boardwalk, climbing moderately through fields of wildflowers above the Logan Pass Visitor Center. It tops out at Hidden Lake Pass in the shadow of Mount Clements. From the pass, Mount Reynolds dominates the southern skyline, while Bearhat Mountain rises on the far side of islet-strewn Hidden Lake. About 0.3 mile farther is an overlook point, from which the trail descends almost 700 feet to the north shore of the lake. Hidden Lake is reputed to contain large but wary cutthroat trout, which offer challenging angling.

Hidden Lake

9
HAYSTACK BUTTE

Type of hike: Out-and-back.
Total distance: 6.8 miles (round trip).
Time required: 3 to 6 hours.
Elevation change: 200-foot loss, 600-foot gain to Haystack Butte.
Finding the trailhead: The trail begins at Logan Pass, across the highway from the visitor center.

The hike: This section of the Highline Trail is one of the most popular hikes in the park, owing to its spectacular vistas, excellent wildlife viewing opportunities, and low level of difficulty. The trail follows the west face of the Continental Divide, maintaining a relatively constant elevation. The Highline Trail crosses excellent habitat for many types of wildlife, and the open subalpine meadows of the Garden Wall allow easy viewing of wild creatures in their natural environments. Columbia ground squirrels abound in the alpine tundra, and hoary marmots and pikas live among the boulders of talus slopes. Look for mountain goats and bighorn sheep near the bases of the cliffs and among stands of fir. Raptors often soar on thermals high above the alpine meadows, hunting for rodents. Please do not feed the wildlife, in the interest of keeping it wild.

The trail begins at Logan Pass, winding through twisted forms of subalpine firs and Engelmann spruce. Strong

Haystack Butte

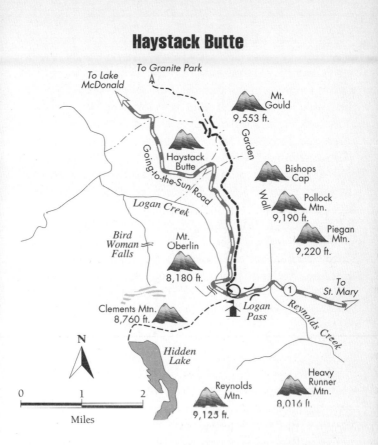

winter winds blow ice particles that tear the branches from the windward side of the trees, giving them a flag-like appearance. In areas of especially high wind, all exposed branches may be pruned by windblown ice, creating a low, mat-like growth form called krummholz in adult spruce and firs. Watch for mountain goats here.

After several hundred yards, the trail winds around a sheer cliff face, high above the valley below. There is a cable handrail for nervous travelers. The trail then continues northward through open stands of fir, following in the shadow of the Garden Wall. This landform was created by the action of glaciers moving down valleys on both sides of a mountain mass. The resulting knife-edge ridge is called an *arête*. Winter avalanches hurtle down from its heights on a regular basis, clearing broad swaths in the trees and shrubs. Across the valley, mounts Oberlin, Clements, and Cannon cradle a high-hanging basin, formed by glaciers, from which Bird Woman Falls cascades almost 500 feet to the valley floor.

The path soon levels off for a long stretch, proceeding northward beneath the towering cliffs. Views now expand to include Heavens Peak to the northwest, and soon there are views of the rest of the Livingston Range stretching away into Canada. The trail ultimately emerges into an open bowl clad in tundra. Bear grass and other wildflowers bloom here beside slender rills and stairstep cascades. The trail climbs gently to the pass behind Haystack Butte, a rounded promontory that juts into the Logan Creek valley. Golden-mantled ground squirrels, identified by the alternating stripes of black and blond on their backs, inhabit the slopes around Haystack Butte. From here there are fine views southward to Logan Pass, with Mount Reynolds presiding over it and a slender skein of water descending into the valley below. This is the turnaround point, and it makes an ideal lunch spot. Huge boulders have fallen into the saddle from the cliffs above; rest on a rock to avoid damaging the fragile vegetation.

10
ST. MARY AND VIRGINIA FALLS

Type of hike: Out-and-back.
Total distance: 2.4 miles round-trip to St. Mary Falls; 3.6 miles round-trip to Virginia Falls.
Time required: 1.5 to 3.5 hours, depending on destination.
Elevation change: 260-foot loss, 285-foot gain.
Finding the trailhead: The trailhead is located on the Going-to-the-Sun Road, about 0.3 mile west of Baring Creek.

Key points:
0.0   Trail sign. Trail descends toward the St. Mary River.
0.3   Junction with the Piegan Pass trail. Turn right for St. Mary Falls and Virginia Falls.
0.7   Junction with St. Mary trail. Turn left for falls.
1.2   Trail crosses St. Mary River at St. Mary Falls. Trail continues, ascending the south side of the St. Mary valley.
1.8   Virginia Falls.

The hike: This trail is a short and pleasant stroll through sun-dappled forest to several roaring waterfalls in the valley below Going-to-the-Sun Road. From the trailhead, the trail descends to the valley floor, past well-marked trail junctions, to cross the river immediately below the thundering cataract of St. Mary Falls. Beyond the falls the forest opens up,

43

St. Mary and Virgina Falls

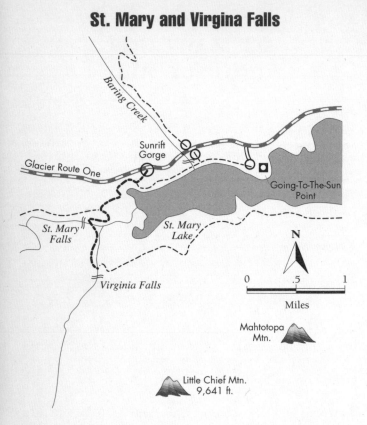

affording views of Little Chief and Dusty Star mountains. The path winds around the ends of several hillocks to reach Virginia Creek, which it follows for 0.5 mile past a narrow gorge. The hike ends at equally impressive Virginia Falls, which emerges from the mouth of a hanging valley.

11
SUN POINT NATURE TRAIL

Type of hike: Out-and-back.
Total distance: 1.3 miles (round trip).
Time required: 45 minutes to 1.5 hours.
Elevation change: Minimal.
Finding the trailhead: The trail begins from the Sun Point parking area, 11 miles east of Logan Pass on Going-to-the-Sun Road.

The hike: This short trek offers excellent views of St. Mary Lake, with a stunning waterfall at the end of the hike. It is a self-guiding nature trail with pamphlets available at the beginning of the trail.

The hike begins by dipping to reach a fork in the trail. Bear left on a spur path to make the short climb to Sun Point, which overlooks St. Mary Lake. A sign points out the names of the massive summits that ring the lake. These summits have a reddish cast because they are composed of Grinnell argillite, a mudstone that is rich in iron and turns red as the iron oxidizes. During the uplift that created the Rocky Mountains some 65 million years ago, these old sea-floor sediments were tilted skyward, and the direction of the tilt can be seen today in the slant of the rock strata.

Return to the main trail and hike westward as it runs level above the shores of St. Mary Lake. A sparse growth of wind-torn lodgepole pines allows fine views of the water and the peaks that surround it. The turquoise, glacier-fed

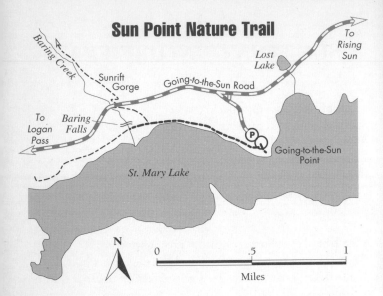

Sun Point Nature Trail

Baring Creek

To Rising Sun

Lost Lake

Sunrift Gorge

Going-to-the-Sun Road

To Logan Pass

Baring Falls

P

Going-to-the-Sun Point

St. Mary Lake

N

0 .5 1

Miles

lake is almost 300 feet deep, occupying a basin that was carved out by a massive valley glacier during the Pleistocene Epoch. The ice was so deep that it reached the tops of the highest summits. The U-shaped cross-section of the valley is the telltale footprint of the long-vanished glacier. As the path crosses sliderock beneath a low cliff, note the green bedrock. This is Appekuny argillite, older than the Grinnell formation but made of a similar mudstone.

The path enters a woodland of spruce and Douglas-fir as it approaches Baring Creek. Bear left at the junction as the main trail crosses a footlog to reach the base of Baring Falls. This impressive cascade drops across a sheer cliff of argillite into a natural amphitheater in the rock. Turn around here and retrace your steps to complete the hike.

12
BEAVER POND TRAIL

Type of hike: Loop.
Total distance: 3.4 miles.
Time required: 1.5 to 3 hours.
Elevation change: 120-foot gain.
Finding the trailhead: Take Going-to-the-Sun Road 0.25 mile east from St. Mary to a paved road entering on the south before the park entrance station. Take this road, bearing right, about 0.5 mile to a parking lot with a trailhead sign. Hike up to the old St. Mary Ranger Station, which was built in 1910, to begin the loop.

Key points:
0.1   Old St. Mary Ranger Station. Trail departs behind the buildings.
1.3   Beaver pond.
1.8   Junction with Red Eagle Trail. Turn right onto old road.
3.4   Old roadbed returns to trailhead.

The hike: Though lacking in spectacular scenery, this hike runs through a pleasant landscape of coniferous forests, grassy meadows, and aspen groves. It receives few visitors and is thus a good place to find solitude.

The trail begins by climbing the hill to the original St. Mary Ranger Station, built in 1910 of native timber. Behind the old buildings, the path ascends to a low ridgetop

Beaver Pond Trail

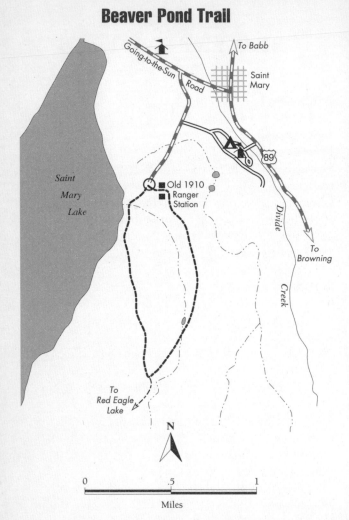

To Babb

Going-to-the-Sun Road

Saint Mary

89

Saint Mary Lake

Old 1910 Ranger Station

Divide Creek

To Browning

To Red Eagle Lake

N

| 0 | .5 | 1 |

Miles

that bears the scars of periodic lightning fires. This ridge is a terminal moraine of the glacier that carved the St. Mary valley, bulldozed into place at the toe of the glacier by the slow but inexorable surge of glacial ice. The path follows the ridgetop through shady stands of Douglas-fir and grassy meadows, providing views of Red Eagle Mountain to the southwest and East Flattop Mountain to the north. Eventually the woodland opens onto rank grasslands bordered by aspen groves, and Split Mountain appears up the Red Eagle Creek valley.

The trail soon reaches a stagnant pond dammed by beavers. The beavers are long gone, but their pond is a good spot to look for birdlife. The trail then turns west and descends to abandoned Red Eagle Road, now a hiking trail. Turn right as the old road parallels the shore of St. Mary Lake, yielding occasional views of the water. The roadbed bears travelers back to the parking lot to complete the loop.

The Two Medicine Valley

OVERVIEW

The mountains of the Two Medicine area were known to the Blackfeet Indians as "the Backbone of the World." They used the area for vision quests as well as hunting and gathering. The towering spires and sheer cliffs still provoke awe in travelers searching for a haven from the hurried pace of the modern world. A well-worn network of trails here provides access to a landscape of unequaled beauty, visiting peaceful lakes and dizzying heights.

In this eastern part of the park, sheer mountains rise abruptly from the rolling Great Plains, providing a mixture of flora and fauna from widely different biotic communities. The alpine communities of higher elevations grade into grasslands adapted to the more arid plains. Since the mountains of the divide form a barrier to moisture-laden maritime air masses, this area occupies a rain shadow. Precipitation on the plains falls mostly in summer in the form of brief thunderstorms, following the rainfall regime of the high plains. This pattern of precipitation favors shallow-rooted grasses over larger trees and shrubs, thus accounting for the lack of lush forests on this side of the divide.

Area wildlife reflects the drier vegetation. Bighorn sheep, favoring grasses as forage, are seen more commonly in this drier area than are mountain goats. Golden eagles soar on updrafts created by the warmth of the sun on open grasslands. Waterfalls block the immigration of native fish

The Two Medicine Valley

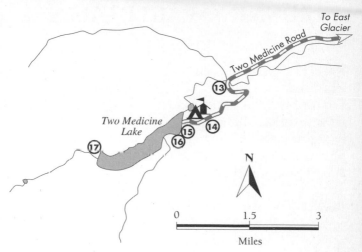

into most of the high lakes; fish found in most of these lakes were introduced at some time in the past. These planted fish have successfully made a place for themselves in the lake ecosystems and now sustain their populations naturally, without supplementary plantings by the National Park Service.

Dry winds roar through the high mountain passes here, a dominant force in shaping the patterns of vegetation in the Front Range. These same winds reach speeds upwards of 80 miles per hour and cause incredibly high wind-chill factors in winter.

13
RUNNING EAGLE FALLS

Type of hike: Out-and-back.
Total distance: 0.6 mile (round trip).
Time required: 15 to 45 minutes.
Elevation change: Minimal.
Finding the trailhead: The trail begins at the Red Eagle Falls parking area, on the north side of Two Medicine Road about 2 miles past the park entrance station.

The hike: This short stroll leads to an odd waterfall that emerges from an underground cave during late summer but pours over a higher sill during spring runoff. There are plans in the works to pave the trail and make it accessible to wheelchairs as far as the banks of Two Medicine Creek.

The walk begins in an open woodland of spruce and fir underlain by a vigorous growth of shrubs. A few old cottonwoods date from floods in years past. Cottonwood seedlings require bare soil and plenty of groundwater to get established, a combination that is unique to rivers that scour their banks with periodic floods. The two major peaks that are visible along the way are Rising Wolf Mountain to the northwest and Spot Mountain to the northeast. The path soon reaches a broad stretch of bare gravel where the Dry Fork joins the Two Medicine River. The Dry Fork floods each spring during snowmelt season, and the force of these

Running Eagle Falls

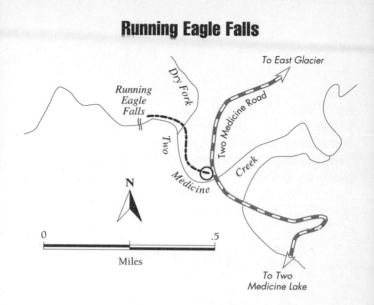

periodic deluges is sufficient to sweep the banks bare of vegetation.

After crossing a footbridge over the river, the path climbs to an overlook below Running Eagle Falls. This unique cataract pours over a sill of stone 40 feet high during early summer. But when the river level drops, the upper channel dries up and the falls emerge from a hidden grotto some 20 feet below the upper lip. This odd phenomenon led early visitors to nickname the site "Trick Falls." A rough and uneven path closes the remaining distance to the foot of the falls, which thunder into a placid pool of deep turquoise water.

14
APPISTOKI FALLS

Type of hike: Out-and-back.
Total distance: 1.2 miles, round-trip.
Time required: 30 to 60 minutes.
Elevation change: 320-foot gain.
Finding the trailhead: Trail departs from the marked Scenic Point Trailhead on the Two Medicine Road, about 4 miles beyond the park entrance station.

Appistoki Falls

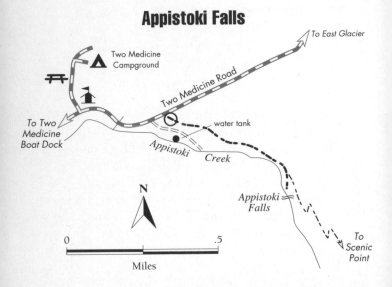

The hike: This trail climbs to a small waterfall in the barren gorge of Appistoki Creek. It begins in a pleasant woodland of subalpine fir, lit by the blossoms of bear grass in early summer of favorable years. Bear grass is not a grass at all but a member of the lily family, with great bulb-shaped clusters of tiny white flowers. It blooms on a three-year cycle, with most plants in a given locale coming into bloom during the same year. The path rises gently through the forest, which thins with increasing elevation. The barren face of Appistoki Peak looms to the west, while the similar summit of Scenic Point rises to the east.

The trail strikes Appistoki Creek at the base of the mountains as it emerges from a desolate vale between the peaks. Turn right at the junction to reach an overlook on the rim of a rocky ravine. From here, the main waterfall can be seen as it slides down across an inclined face of stone, with pools and lesser cascades below it.

15
TWO MEDICINE LAKE

Type of hike: Loop.
Total distance: 7.4 miles with no side trips.
Time required: 4 to 7 hours.
Elevation change: 340-foot gain and loss.
Finding the trailhead: The loop begins at Two Medicine Lake's South Shore Trailhead, at the west end of the Two Medicine boat dock parking lot. The hike ends at Two Medicine Campground. Boat users may enter the trail system at the lake's upper boat dock.

Key points:
0.0   South Shore Trailhead.
0.2   Junction with Paradise Point spur (0.4 mile). Bear left for loop.
1.2   Junction with Aster Park trail. Bear right for loop.
2.2   Bridge over Paradise Creek.
2.3   Junction with Cobalt Lake Trail. Turn right.
3.3   Junction with boat dock trail. Turn left.
3.9   Junction with Upper Two Medicine Trail. Turn right onto Dawson cutoff trail.
4.1   Junction with Dawson Pass Trail. Turn right to complete loop.
7.4   Trail crosses bridge below Pray Lake to end at Two Medicine Campground.

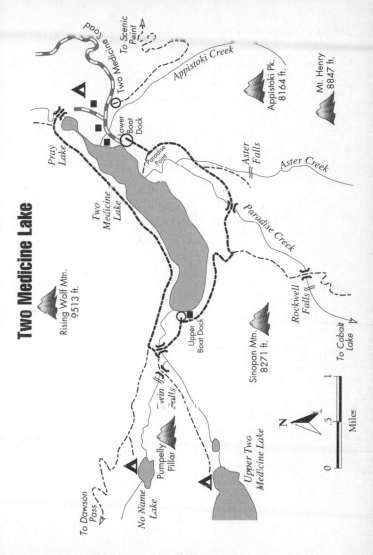

Two Medicine Lake

Rising Wolf Mtn. 9513 ft.

Pray Lake

Two Medicine Lake

To Two Medicine

To Scenic Point

Appistoki Creek

Appistoki Pk. 8164 ft.

Mt. Henry 8847 ft.

Lower Boat Dock

Paradise Point

Aster Falls

Aster Creek

Paradise Creek

Rockwell Falls

Upper Boat Dock

Sinopan Mtn. 8271 ft.

To Cobalt Lake

Twin Falls

Pumpelly Pillar

N

Mile

0   .5   1

To Dawson Pass

No Name Lake

Upper Two Medicine Lake

57

The hike: This trail makes a circuit around Two Medicine Lake. It travels inland for most of its length, but offers periodic views of the water and the glacier-carved peaks that surround it. The loop requires a full day of traveling for most folks; if you are less ambitious, you might opt to hike out to Paradise Point for fine views, or take the tour boat to the head of the lake and hike one of the legs of the loop back to your vehicle.

The hike begins with a modest climb into subalpine firs south of Two Medicine Lake. At the top of the rise is an intersection; here, a spur path descends to Paradise Point on the lakeshore. This nice side trip drops through the trees, then crosses rank meadows to reach the tip of the headland. Paradise Point is the tip of an alluvial fan, built up as sediments carried down from the mountains by Paradise Creek poured into the lake and settled out as the water lost its speed. A gravel beach offers outstanding views of the surrounding peaks without the crowds that throng the foot of the lake.

Meanwhile, the main trail wanders inland, passing old beaver ponds and wetlands. Open meadows beside the marshes offer outstanding views of Appistoki Peak and Never Laughs Mountain to the south, Sinopah Mountain above the head of the lake, and Rising Wolf Mountain beyond the far shore. A footbridge leads across Aster Creek, and on the far bank a spur trail spans the short distance to Aster Falls then climbs steadily to the Aster Park overlook.

The Two Medicine loop now charts a level westward course through a loose woodland of fir and pine, ultimately crossing a suspension bridge at Paradise Creek. This substantial stream riffles through picturesque channels in the slanted bedrock. On its far bank is a junction; bear right as the path skirts the foot of Sinopah Mountain. As the trail winds around the north face of Sinopah, it crosses avalanche slopes that offer fine views of the lake. Be alert for grizzly bears in this area.

A steady descent leads into the spruce forest at the head of the lake. Here, a short stroll leads down to the boat dock while the loop route leads westward. The spruce trees soon thin out, and Pumpelly Pillar can be seen ahead. After crossing the headwaters of the Two Medicine River, the trail reaches an intersection near Twin Falls. Turn left to visit the falls, a double cascade that descends from the Bighorn Basin, or turn right to complete the loop.

The main trail follows signs for Dawson Pass as it runs eastward with fine views of the Pumpelly Pillar and Sinopah Mountain. After linking up with the trail from Dawson Pass, the path ascends southward onto an alluvial fan at the base of Rising Wolf Mountain. From here hikers get superb views of the lake, as well as Appistoki Peak and Never Laughs Mountain beyond it. The trail then glides down into lakeshore forest and doesn't emerge again until it reaches the foot of the lake. Follow the trail around Pray Lake to reach the bridge leading to Two Medicine Campground and the end of the hike.

16
ASTER PARK

Type of hike: Out-and-back.
Total distance: A 3.8 mile round trip.
Time required: 2 to 4 hours.
Elevation change: 440-foot gain.
Finding the trailhead: The hike begins at the Two Medicine Lake South Shore Trailhead, located at the west end of the Two Medicine boat dock parking lot.

Key points:

0.0   South Shore Trailhead.
0.2   Junction with Paradise Point spur (0.4 mile). Bear left for loop.
1.2   Junction with Aster Park Trail. Turn left.
1.3   Spur trail to base of Aster Falls.
1.9   Aster Park overlook.

The hike: This route combines the early reaches of the Two Medicine Loop with a spur trail that visits a pretty waterfall then climbs to a high overlook above Two Medicine Lake.

The hike begins by climbing gently into subalpine forest south of Two Medicine Lake. At the top of the rise is a trail junction, where a spur path descends to Paradise Point on the lakeshore. The main trail wanders inland, passing stagnant wetlands; open meadows beside the marshes offer

Aster Park

Two Medicine Campground

To East Glacier

Two Medicine Rd.

Boat Dock

Paradise Point

Two Medicine Lake

Paradise Creek

Aster Falls

Aster Creek

Overlook

N

0   .5   1

Miles

outstanding views of Appistoki Peak and Never Laughs Mountain to the south, Sinopah Mountain above the head of the lake, and Rising Wolf Mountain beyond the far shore. A footbridge leads across Aster Creek, and on the far bank is the junction with the Aster Park trail.

Turn left as this spur trail rises gently through the pines and firs. Soon a side path splits away toward the base of Aster Falls, where Aster Creek sluices down through a cleft in the bedrock, arcing downward in ribbonlike streams. The main trail makes several upward switchbacks, then settles into a steady westward grade through the trees. At the top of a low headwall, hikers will get fine aerial views of Two Medicine Lake and the surrounding crags. The trail then turns south into the hanging valley of Aster Creek before climbing to its end on a rocky overlook at the edge of the Two Medicine valley.

17
UPPER TWO MEDICINE LAKE

Type of hike: Out-and-back.
Total distance: 4.4 miles, round trip with boat shuttle.
Time required: 2 to 3 hours.
Elevation change: 440-foot gain.
Finding the trailhead: Ferry travelers will begin the hike at the Upper Two Medicine boat dock. Hikers intending to walk the whole way will begin at the South Shore Trailhead, located at the west end of the Two Medicine boat dock parking lot, and follow the route described under "Two Medicine Lake (Hike 15)."

Key points:
0.0 Upper Two Medicine boat dock.
0.1 Junction with South Shore Trail. Bear right.
0.7 Junction with Dawson cutoff trail. Bear left.
0.9 Spur trail to Twin Falls (0.2 mile). Bear left for Upper Two Medicine Lake.
2.2 Upper Two Medicine Lake.

The hike: Visitors can combine this spur trail with the Two Medicine Loop for a long day hike of 10.4 miles, or take the tour boat to the head of Two Medicine Lake and hike the trail in a couple of hours. If you do take the boat, be sure to find out when scheduled boat trips depart for the return trip to the foot of the lake.

Upper Two Medicine Lake

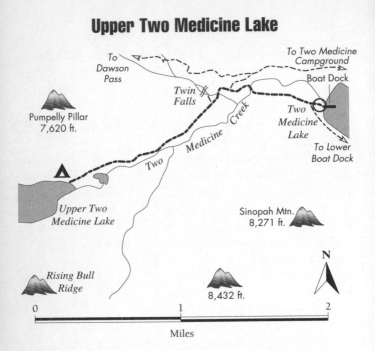

From the boat dock, the trail climbs gently through a bottomland forest of spruce. The trees soon thin, and Pumpelly Pillar rises ahead. After crossing the headwaters of the Two Medicine River, the trail reaches an intersection; turn left here for Upper Two Medicine Lake. Just a short distance farther, a spur path leads northward to the base of Twin Falls. These paired cascades descend across a rocky face from their origin in the Bighorn Basin.

Meanwhile, the main trail crosses the creek below the falls and continues its gentle climb up the valley. Where it rises onto the slopes below the cliffs of Pumpelly Pillar, avalanches have cleared away the trees to reveal Mount Rockwell across the valley, as well as the gabled cliffs above the trail. The track soon passes a shallow tarn, then gradually ascends to the foot of Upper Two Medicine Lake. This long, sinuous lake is flanked by glacier-carved walls, and Lone Walker Mountain presides above its head.

Many Glacier

OVERVIEW

Many Glacier Hotel was built in 1914 by the Great Northern Railway as a destination resort for its rail tourists. The hotel sits among soaring peaks and jagged arêtes that give this area the nickname "America's Little Switzerland." Since the park's creation, a myriad of trails have been built to reach the scenic wonders surrounding the hotel, making the Many Glacier area a hub for day-hiking activities. Lush meadows and tumbling waterfalls below snowy peaks invite the traveler to pause and contemplate the awe-inspiring beauty of the mountains.

The lower end of the valley is dominated by Lake Sherburne, which was impounded during the early 1920s. The formation of this reservoir inundated the old mining town of Altyn, which had once served as a center for unsuccessful gold and copper operations in the surrounding mountains, as well as an oil boondoggle.

The Many Glacier area is home to many kinds of wildlife. Most prominent is the majestic grizzly bear, frequently seen foraging for bulbs and berries on the open slopes of the surrounding mountains. Mountain goats cavort on the rocky ledges of cliffs, and bighorn sheep ewes with their young sometimes appear in the lowlands around the hotel. The meadows and forests abound with rodents and songbirds of all kinds.

Visitor services are available in the area around the hotel as well as in the nearby town of Babb, on the neighboring Blackfeet Indian Reservation. Trail rides of varying duration depart from the Many Glacier corral above the hotel, and a privately owned tour boat runs between the hotel and the upper end of Lake Josephine, providing interpretive tours and transportation to the upper Cataract Creek drainage. The spacious campground at Many Glacier provides sites for all types of vehicles.

Many Glacier

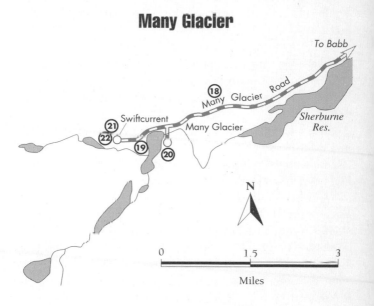

18
APIKUNI FALLS

Type of hike: Out-and-back.
Total distance: 2 miles, round-trip.
Time required: 1 to 2 hours.
Elevation change: 680-foot gain.
Finding the trailhead: Trail begins at the Apikuni Falls Trailhead, 3.3 miles west of the Many Glacier Entrance Station.

The hike: This short, steep trail leads up to the desolate cliffs of Apikuni Mountain to visit a long and slender waterfall. Hikers will get excellent mountain views throughout the trek.

The hike begins on Apikuni Flats, where grassy meadows offer views of the major peaks up the valley: Mount Gould, with its chiseled countenance; the symmetrical pyramid of Grinnell Point to the north of it; and, between them, the Garden Wall, graced with Salamander and Grinnell glaciers. At the far edge of the flats, the path undertakes a relentless and calf-burning climb, passing through aspen groves and lodgepole pine stands as it ascends to the base of limestone cliffs. Altyn Peak rises west of Apikuni Creek, while the outer bulwarks of Apikuni Mountain (its reddish summit can be seen through the mouth of the hanging valley above) rise to the east.

The path ultimately climbs onto rocky and barren slopes where only a few firs survive, and the bleached and gnarled

Apikuni Falls

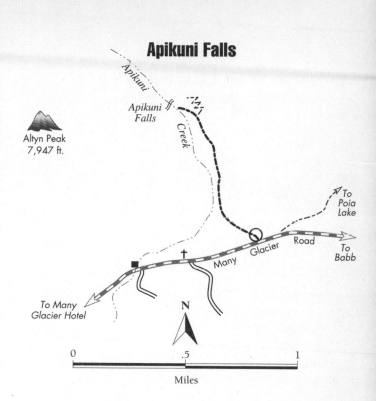

Apikuni

Apikuni
Falls

Altyn Peak
7,947 ft.

Creek

To
Poia
Lake

Glacier   Road

To
Babb

Many

To Many
Glacier Hotel

N

0   .5   1

Miles

skeletons of long-dead whitebark pines rise mournfully to
the sky. Swiftcurrent Lake and Lake Josephine can now be
glimpsed in the valley to the west, while to the south a broad
panorama includes Wynn and Allen mountains arrayed beyond Sherburne Reservoir. Apikuni Falls can be seen ahead,
dropping through a cleft in the limestone walls. The path
becomes primitive with steep, uneven footing as it navigates
a rocky ravine to reach the base of the falls.

19
SWIFTCURRENT NATURE TRAIL

Type of hike: Loop.
Total distance: 2.5 miles.
Time required: 1 to 2 hours.
Elevation change: Minimal.
Finding the trailhead: Follow Many Glacier Road past the hotel access road to reach the picnic area at the northwest corner of Swiftcurrent Lake. The trail begins here.

Key points:
0.0   Picnic area at northwest corner of Swiftcurrent Lake.
0.8   Upper boat dock.
1.5   Many Glacier Hotel. Follow promenade along lakeshore.
1.9   Junction with Ptarmigan Tunnel Trail. Stay left as loop trail follows lakeshore.
2.5   Trail returns to picnic area.

The hike: This self-guided nature walk makes a circuit around Swiftcurrent Lake. The scenery is spectacular, but hikers will walk past the Many Glacier Hotel and along several roadways, so this is not a wilderness hike. Pamphlets interpreting the landscape are available at the trailhead.

From the picnic area, hike southward as the trail crosses the braided channels of Swiftcurrent Creek. The stream is

Swiftcurrent Nature Trail

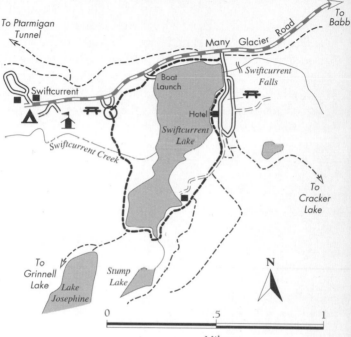

bordered by a low growth of willows, which thrive in saturated soils. The trail soon enters a lakeshore woodland of subalpine fir and lodgepole pine. Allen Mountain is the prominent peak to the south, with Wynn Mountain to the left of it. After passing the boat dock, the trail crosses

Grinnell Creek and winds onto the south shore of the lake. The massive summit of Altyn Peak now rises to the north. The forest soon thins, and the trail breaks out of it entirely as it reaches Many Glacier Hotel. Spectacular views now encompass Mount Gould to the west, Grinnell Point above the head of the lake, and Mount Wilbur to the northwest. As you follow the lakeshore promenade, scan the lower slopes of Altyn Peak for grizzly bears and bighorn sheep. The trail now runs beside the road, following the lakeshore as it bends westward to return to the picnic area.

20
GRINNELL LAKE

Type of hike: Out-and-back.
Total distance: 6.8 miles (round trip) on foot; 1.9 miles (round trip) with boat shuttle.
Time required: 3.5 to 7 hours on foot, 1 to 1.5 hours with boat (hiking time only).
Elevation change: 120-foot gain.
Finding the trailhead: The trail begins from the southwest corner of the parking lot above Many Glacier Hotel.

Key points:

0.0	Many Glacier Hotel parking lot.
0.2	Trail crosses access road to boat dock.
0.6	Trail crosses Grinnell Creek.
0.7	Upper boat dock on Swiftcurrent Lake. Turn left, following signs for Lake Josephine.
0.8	Trail reaches south shore of Lake Josephine. Bear right.
1.8	Junction with Grinnell Glacier Trail. Stay left.
2.2	Junction with Grinnell Glacier cutoff. Bear left to cross Grinnell Creek.
2.5	Junction with boat dock trail. Turn right. Tour boat users start hike here.
3.4	Grinnell Lake.

The hike: This trail visits a glacier-fed lake at the base of a stunning waterfall. The lake is reached most easily by

Grinnell Lake

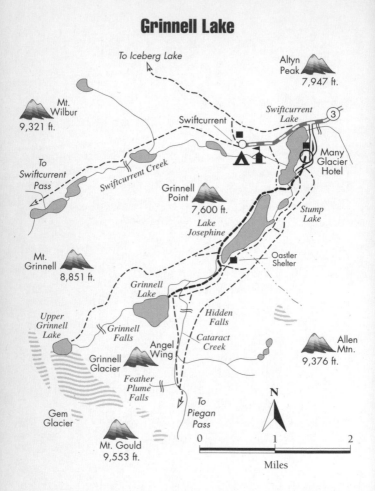

To Iceberg Lake

Altyn
Peak
7,947 ft.

Mt.
Wilbur
9,321 ft.

Swiftcurrent
Lake

3

Swiftcurrent

To
Swiftcurrent
Pass

Swiftcurrent Creek

Many
Glacier
Hotel

Grinnell
Point
7,600 ft.

Stump
Lake

Lake
Josephine

Mt.
Grinnell
8,851 ft.

Oastler
Shelter

Grinnell
Lake

Hidden
Falls

Upper
Grinnell
Lake

Grinnell
Falls

Cataract
Creek

Allen
Mtn.
9,376 ft.

Angel
Wing

Grinnell
Glacier

Feather
Plume
Falls

To
Piegan
Pass

N

Gem
Glacier

0   1   2

Mt. Gould
9,553 ft.

Miles

taking a tour boat across Swiftcurrent Lake and Lake Josephine; hikers who take the tour boat can skip the next two paragraphs. More adventurous hikers can walk through a spectacular mountain landscape past these two lakes to reach the upper boat dock and hook up with the Grinnell Lake Trail. Rangers offer guided interpretive trips to Grinnell Lake via the tour boat on an occasional basis.

From the Many Glacier Hotel parking lot, follow the leg of the Swiftcurrent Nature Trail that crosses the road to the boat dock and then follows the southern shoreline of Swiftcurrent Lake. Subalpine firs form a loose woodland here, and many openings offer views of the surrounding peaks. Grinnell Point is the pyramid-shaped horn that guards the head of the lake, while to the left of it is the grand and bulky edifice of Mount Gould. Farther north, the graceful fin of Mount Wilbur rises above the Swiftcurrent Creek valley. As the trail approaches the spot where Cataract Creek pours into the head of the lake, watch for the bulky massif of Altyn Peak to the northeast.

The path crosses a bridge over Grinnell Creek to reach the Upper Swiftcurrent Boat Dock; turn left here for the short and modest climb through the trees that leads to the foot of Lake Josephine. The route now leads along the north shore of this long, turquoise lake. Frequent avalanches from the slopes of Grinnell Point have cleared away the trees, leaving a lush growth of herbaceous plants. Superb views from the lakeshore are dominated by Mount Gould, with the much smaller summit of Angel Wing Mountain projecting from its west face like a flying buttress. Allen

Mountain rises beyond the opposite shore, draped with slender waterfalls during early summer. After passing a junction with the Grinnell Glacier trail, the main trail runs through a stand of spruce and then swings south to cross the marshy flats above the head of the lake.

At the southwestern corner of the lake, the path is joined by the trail from the boat dock; tour boat travelers begin the hike here. Turn right as the trail runs westward through the deep shade of a spruce woodland that is sheltered from winter gales by the surrounding ridges. The path ultimately makes a final crossing of Grinnell Creek to reach the shores of Grinnell Lake. The luminous aquamarine color of the water is derived from glacial flour, a finely pulverized rock sediment suspended in the lake. As sunlight enters the water, it is diffracted by the suspended silt so that only light in the blue and green parts of the spectrum can escape.

The lake occupies a natural amphitheater at the foot of Angel Wing. On the opposite shore, Grinnell Falls drops 1,000 feet across sheer cliffs, bringing meltwater from Grinnell Glacier into the lake. The pile of gravel above the head of the falls is a terminal moraine pushed into place by a surge of this glacier that took place in the late 1880s. Grinnell Glacier cannot be seen from this spot; the snowfield you see at the base of the peak above the falls is actually the tail of the Salamander Glacier.

21
ICEBERG LAKE

see map on page 80

Type of hike: Out-and-back.
Total distance: 9.1 miles, round-trip.
Time required: 5 to 8 hours.
Elevation change: 1,194-foot gain.
Finding the trailhead: The trail departs from the Iceberg–Ptarmigan Trailhead, at the north end of the Swiftcurrent Motor Lodge complex, among the cabins behind the coffee shop. A parking pullout there is marked with a trailhead sign.

Key points:
0.0   Trail sign.
0.1   Junction with Trail 167. Turn left for Iceberg Lake.
2.3   Trail crosses Ptarmigan Creek at Ptarmigan Falls.
2.4   Junction with Ptarmigan Tunnel trail. Stay left for Iceberg Lake.
4.4   Trail crosses Iceberg Creek below a nameless tarn.
4.5   Iceberg Lake.

The hike: Iceberg Lake is a striking, aquamarine tarn surrounded on three sides by towering cliffs. Ice-out may not occur here until mid-July, and the bergs for which the lake was named may be seen floating about well after that date. This stunning destination plus the brilliant wildflowers along the route make the Iceberg Lake Trail one of the most popular hikes in the park. It crosses fine grizzly bear habitat, and bears are seen frequently on the open slopes on both sides of the trail.

The hike begins as a short connecting trail that climbs briskly for several hundred yards to join the main trail coming in from the hotel. The trail then turns northwest, climbing gently along the open slopes high above Wilbur Creek. Look for the magenta spikes of fireweed and the bulblike inflorescences of beargrass (a member of the lily family) early in the season. The trail passes below Altyn Peak, a greenish massif of Appekuny argillite. Mount Wilbur, known to the Blackfeet people as "Heavy Shield Mountain," rises across the valley to the south. The trail passes into open forests on its way to Ptarmigan Falls, a popular rest stop on hot summer days.

Shortly after passing the falls, the trail reaches the junction with the Ptarmigan Tunnel trail, then turns southwest along the Ptarmigan Wall through increasingly alpine scenery toward the head of the valley. Looking south, hikers can glimpse a waterfall on Iceberg Creek through the trees. The trail climbs gently as it curls south into the glacial cirque that holds Iceberg Lake.

The 3,000-foot cliffs surrounding the lake provide prime escape habitat for mountain goats, which frequent this area. Talus slopes along the lake's south shore are home to a variety of small mammals, including pikas and ground squirrels. The permanent snowfields at the head of the lake are remnants of a glacier that until recently occupied this basin beneath the cool shadows of Iceberg Peak.

22
BULLHEAD LAKE

Type of hike: Out-and-back.
Total distance: 6.6 miles, round-trip.
Time required: 3 to 5 hours.
Elevation change: 240-foot gain.
Finding the trailhead: The trail begins at the west end of the Swiftcurrent Lodge coffee shop parking lot.

Key points:

0.0   Trail sign.
0.2   Junction with horse trail. Stay left for Bullhead Lake. Trail follows floor of Swiftcurrent Valley, climbing gently.
2.0   Redrock Lake.
2.3   Redrock Falls.
3.3   Bullhead Lake.

The hike: This hike follows the Swiftcurrent Valley past a chain of pretty lakes, visiting Redrock Falls along the way. The trail begins at the Swiftcurrent Motor Lodge and winds westward along the valley floor among groves of tall aspen interspersed with lodgepole pine. The cliffs of Grinnell Point rise to the south, and as the trail runs westward, the summit of Grinnell Peak comes into view along the same ridge.

The trail passes north of Fishercap Lake, which can be glimpsed briefly through a few holes in the vegetation. It

Iceberg Lake and Bullhead Lake

Ptarmigan Lake

Crowfeet Mtn.

Ptarmigan Wall

Mt. Henkel

Ahern Pass

Altyn Peak
7,947 ft.

IceBerg Lake

Iceberg Peak

Wilbur Creek

Many Glacier

Mt. Wilbur
9,321 ft.

Windmaker Lake

Fishercap Lake

Swiftcurrent Mountain Lookout

Redrock Lake

Grinnell Point
7,600 ft.

Bullhead Lake

Lake Josephine

Swiftcurrent Pass

Mt. Grinnell
8,851 ft.

Piegan Pass Trail

Granite Park

N

| 0 | 1 | 2 |

Miles

then climbs gently, crossing a small stream on its way to Redrock Lake. An intense fire cleared this area in 1936. Notice that harsh growing conditions have stunted the pines and aspens around the lake. The trail continues west, passing Redrock Falls above the head of the lake. About 2 miles beyond Redrock Lake, the trail reaches Bullhead Lake. A northward glance reveals Mount Wilbur, Iceberg Peak, and the North Swiftcurrent Glacier on the east face of Swiftcurrent Mountain.

Waterton Lake and Vicinity

OVERVIEW

For a relatively small park, Waterton supports a diverse array of plants, wildlife, and landscapes, leading to varied opportunities for hikers. Long before they were protected as an international peace park, these mountains and valleys were frequented by people of the Kootenai and Blackfoot tribes, who hunted bison and gathered wild plants here. The first visitors of European descent to take in these breathtaking landscapes were undoubtedly fur traders and missionaries, who came in the late 1850s. In the late 1800s, the discovery of oil in the Cameron Valley drew speculators to establish a drilling operation, which flourished only a short time and is remembered today at Discovery Well historic site. A portion of the present-day park was protected in 1895 as Waterton Lakes Forest Park and later called Kootenai Lakes Forest Reserve.

Protection of this natural treasure was increased in response to the urgings of conservation-minded local residents such as Frederick Godsal and John "Kootenai" Brown. The park was expanded in 1914, then reduced to its present size in 1921. In 1932 an international accord with the United States established the Waterton-Glacier complex as the world's first International Peace Park. The ensuing years have

Waterton Lake and Vicinity

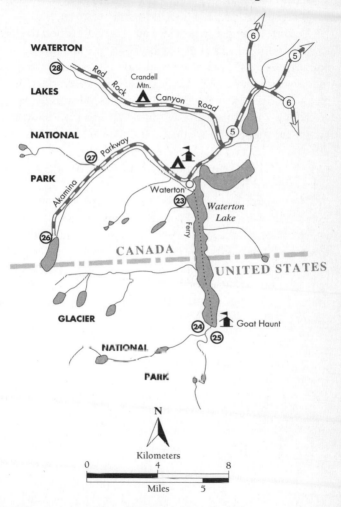

seen extensive development, highlighted by a complex network of trails, roads, and campgrounds. However, the land beyond the roads retains its wild character.

Waterton township provides most services found in large towns, including a variety of hotel accommodations, restaurants, and stores. There are automobile campgrounds at the townsite and along the Red Rock Parkway; developed picnic facilities exist along all major roads. Motorized boats are allowed in Upper and Middle Waterton lakes, and all lakes have facilities for launching unpowered boats. In addition, a water taxi on Upper Waterton Lake provides daily service to Crypt Landing and Goat Haunt Ranger Station across the border.

No registration is required for day trips, but overnight expeditions into the backcountry require a special permit, which can be purchased at the visitor center outside Waterton townsite. Backpackers must stay in established campgrounds, although minimum-impact camping in some remote areas may be allowed by special permit. Fishing in the park requires a special license, available for a small fee at the visitor center.

23
LOWER BERTHA FALLS

Type of hike: Out-and-back.
Total distance: 3.8 miles (6.1km), round-trip.
Time required: 2 to 3.5 hours.
Elevation change: 700-foot (215-meter) gain.
Finding the trailhead: The trail begins in the southwest corner of Waterton townsite, across from the automobile campground. The trailhead is marked by a sign for Bertha Lake, and has its own parking lot.

Key points:
0.0   Trail sign.
0.9   Junction with Waterton Lake Trail. Stay right for Bertha Lake.
1.9   Lower Bertha Falls. End of self-guiding nature trail.

The hike: This popular day hike along Waterton Lake offers interpretive signs along the route, explaining the ecology of the ever changing forest. At the end of the trek is the graceful veil of Lower Bertha Falls.

The trail begins in a stand of aspens, climbing gradually as it follows the western shore of Waterton Lake. As the trail rises above the lakeshore, it crosses a mixed forest of lodgepole pine, fir, and mountain maple. Rocky outcrops are home to limber pine, which thrives in extreme

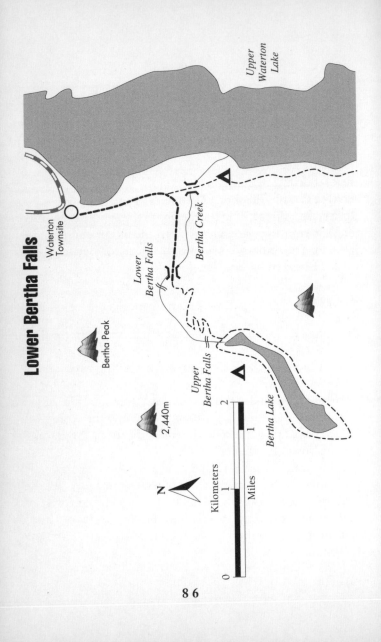

Lower Bertha Falls

Waterton Townsite

Upper Waterton Lake

Bertha Creek

Lower Bertha Falls

Bertha Peak

Upper Bertha Falls

2,440m

Bertha Lake

N

Kilometers
Miles

0   1   2

environments. An overlook about 1 mile down the trail offers sweeping views of the ranges east of the lake, as far south as Mount Cleveland across the international border. At 10,466 feet above sea level, this summit is the loftiest in either park.

Just beyond this overlook, the Bertha Lake trail splits off from the main trail that runs along the shores of Waterton Lake. A left turn here yields a steep 0.5-mile descent to the Bertha Bay Campground. Turn right on the Bertha Lake trail. It bends west, entering the bear grass–studded Bertha Creek valley. After a distance of a mile, the trail reaches the foot of Lower Bertha Falls. Here, Bertha Creek cascades across layers of resistant rock, tumbling into a rushing flume created by a joint in the bedrock. This spot is a nice place for a picnic and marks the end of the easy day hike. Ambitious travelers can continue up the trail another 1.6 miles (2.5 km) and 780 feet (245 m) to reach the shore of Bertha Lake.

24
RAINBOW FALLS

Type of hike: Out-and-back.
Total distance: 1.5 miles, round-trip.
Time required: 45 minutes to 1.5 hours
Elevation change: Minimal.
Finding the trailhead: The trail starts at Goat Haunt Ranger Station, reached by ferry from Waterton townsite or by trail along the western shore of Waterton Lake. The trailhead is located next to the stables, south of the ranger station.

Key points:
0.0   Trail sign behind stables. Follow Waterton Lake Trail.
0.2   Junction with Rainbow Falls spur on near bank of Waterton River. Turn left.
0.7   Rainbow Falls.

The hike: This well-maintained trail is a popular stroll for visitors who take the boat tour on Waterton Lake. The hike begins on the Waterton Lake Trail, which runs westward from Goat Haunt Ranger Station. Barren summits of sedimentary rock flank both sides of Waterton Lake. As the trail nears the Waterton River, bear left on the hiker trail, then turn left at a marked junction with the Rainbow Falls spur trail. This path wanders up the east bank of the river, which is bordered by dense thickets of willow, a favorite

Rainbow Falls

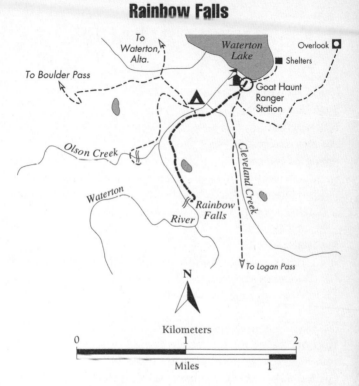

winter forage of moose. After 0.5 mile, the trail reaches Rainbow Falls. Here, the translucent waters of the river foam over a series of low waterfalls.

25
KOOTENAI LAKES

Type of hike: Out-and-back.
Total distance: 5.6 miles, round-trip.
Time required: 3 to 5 hours.
Elevation change: 200-foot gain.
Finding the trailhead: Goat Haunt Ranger Station, reached by ferry from Waterton townsite, or by trail along the western shore of Waterton Lake. The trailhead is located next to the stables, south of the ranger station.

Key points:
0.0   Trail sign. Trail follows the Waterton valley floor.
2.5   Junction with Kootenai Lakes Trail. Turn right.
2.8   Kootenai Lakes.

The hike: This long day hike follows the Waterton Valley Trail up the Waterton River from Goat Haunt Ranger Station, at the head of Waterton Lake. Hikers who attempt this route should catch a boat shuttle early in the morning in order to complete the trip before the last boat of the day departs for Waterton township. Kootenai Lakes provide fishing for good-sized brook trout and the possibility of sighting moose, which frequent the lakes. The lakes also offer backcountry campsites.

After leaving the paved walkways and buildings of the ranger station behind, the trail passes beneath a canopy of

Kootenai Lakes

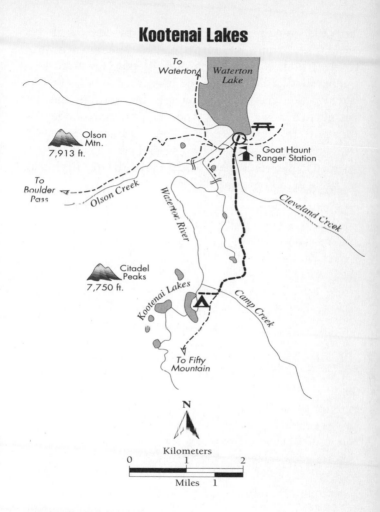

To
Waterton

Waterton
Lake

Olson
Mtn.
7,913 ft.

To
Boulder
Pass

Olson Creek

Goat Haunt
Ranger Station

Waterton River

Cleveland Creek

Citadel
Peaks
7,750 ft.

Kootenai Lakes

Camp Creek

To Fifty
Mountain

N

Kilometers
0   1   2

Miles   1

large old-growth conifers interrupted by occasional wet meadows. At mile 2.5, hikers reach a junction with the Kootenai Lakes Trail, which runs 0.3 mile westward to a campground at the foot of the lower lake. These shallow lakes provide good fishing for large brook trout, and the willows that crowd the shores provide a favored food source for moose, frequently seen here. Forested areas surrounding the lakes are prime habitat for black bears. The lakes are guarded to the west by the Citadel Peaks, the rocky spires at the tail end of Porcupine Ridge.

26
CAMERON LAKE

Type of hike: Out-and-back.
Total distance: 2.2 miles (3.5 km), round-trip.
Elevation change: Minimal.
Finding the trailhead: Follow the paved Cameron Lake Road all the way to its end. The trail starts from a signpost in the lakeshore picnic area.

The hike: This trail runs along the western shore of Cameron Lake, one of the prettiest lakes in the Waterton–Glacier area. A self-guiding pamphlet, available at the trailhead, interprets the ecology of the subalpine forest found along the lake.

From the picnic area, the trail runs through the spruce and fir woodland beside the lake, climbing and falling moderately. As it nears the head of the lake, the trail seeks out a small point where avalanches from Forum Peak have cleared away the trees. Here, hikers get outstanding views of the spectacular Mount Custer headwall and the deep turquoise waters of the lake.

Cameron Lake

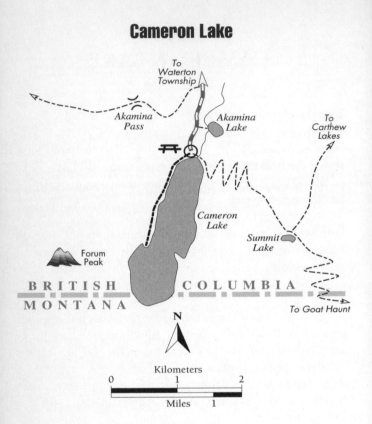

27
LINEHAM FALLS

Type of hike: Out-and-back.
Total distance: 5.2 miles (8.5 km), round-trip.
Time required: 2.5 to 4 hours.
Elevation change: 1,290-foot gain, 130-foot loss.
Finding the trailhead: The trail begins at a marked pullout on the north side of the Cameron Lake Road, just beyond the historic oil well site.

The hike: This pleasant jaunt runs up Lineham Creek to a headwall that rises below a high lake basin. A trail with cable handrails once climbed the headwall with the assistance of cable handrails, but that route has long since been abandoned. The headwall rock is loose and crumbly, and is considered hazardous even by experienced climbers; travelers should not attempt to reach Lineham Lakes via this route.

From the trailhead, our trail takes travelers across wooded flats populated by lodgepole pine and aspen. About 0.25 mile from the road, a steady ascent through the forest takes hikers onto the shoulders of Ruby Ridge as the trail runs westward, high above Lineham Creek. The forest gives way to grassy slopes, and the trail continues to climb as Mount Lineham rises like a lone sentinel across the valley. A backward glance reveals the massive peaks of Buchanan Ridge, which block out the skyline to the east. A mile farther on,

Lineham Falls

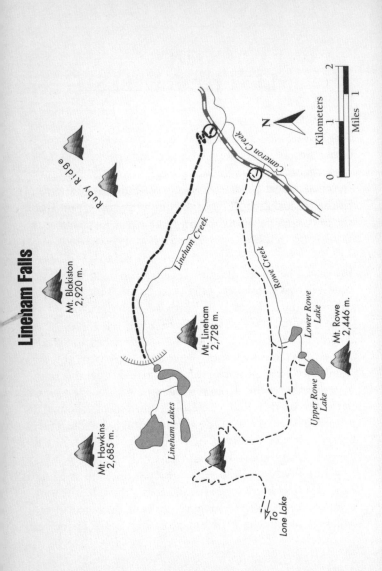

Ruby Ridge

Mt. Blakiston
2,920 m.

Mt. Hawkins
2,685 m.

Lineham Creek

Lineham Lakes

Mt. Lineham
2,728 m.

Rowe Creek

Lower Rowe
Lake

Upper Rowe
Lake

Mt. Rowe
2,446 m.

Cameron Creek

To
Lone Lake

N

Kilometers
0   1   2

Miles
1

the trail enters a forest of tall fir trees and begins to level out. Views are limited to brief glimpses through openings in the forest canopy as the trail tracks west across the soft duff of the forest floor.

Upon entering a broad avalanche path that descends from the rocky face of Mount Blakiston, the trail switchbacks downward about 100 feet to reach the level of the creek. The path meanders beside the stream, which tumbles down a series of cheerful cascades within a narrow canyon. When the trail runs out onto alpine meadows to reach its official terminus, a spur trail runs down to the creek for a clear view of 410-foot Lincham Falls, while a higher path runs uphill for a loftier perspective.

28
BLAKISTON FALLS

Type of hike: Out-and-back.
Total distance: 1.6 miles (2.5 km), round-trip.
Time required: 45 minutes to 1.5 hours.
Elevation change: Minimal.
Finding the trailhead: The trail begins from the Red Rock Canyon parking lot. Cross Red Rock Creek and take a left to descend to the bridge over Bauerman Creek, which is the starting point for the Blakiston Trail.

Key points:
0.0   Trail sign. Take the paved trail across Red Rock Creek, then turn left.
0.2   Bridge over Bauerman Creek.
0.8   Blakiston Falls.

The hike: From the parking lot at Red Rock Canyon, cross Red Rock Creek and turn left, descending along its northwest bank to reach a stout bridge above Bauerman Creek. Mount Blakiston rises to the south, while Anderson Peak is to the west. Once across this bridge, take the right-most trail, which is for hikers. The trail climbs gently through coniferous forest, with views of Mount Blakiston through numerous openings. At Blakiston Falls, the trail passes a wooden observation platform that leans out over the water to provide excellent views of the thundering cascade.

Blakiston Falls

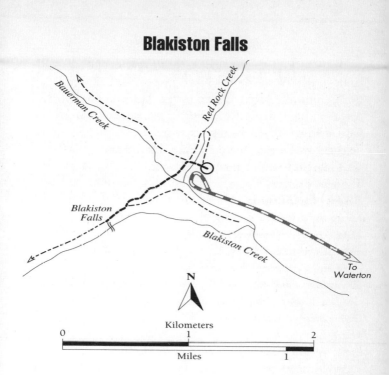

About The Author

Erik Molvar spends half of each year exploring wildlands in the West. He has hiked more than 8,000 miles of trails, from the Arctic Ocean to the Mexican border. Erik has a master's degree in wildlife management from the University of Alaska Fairbanks, where he researched moose behavior in Denali National Park. He currently resides in the Gallatin River country of Montana.

Also by this author:

Hiking the North Cascades
Best Easy Day Hikes—North Cascades
Hiking Olympic National Park
Best Easy Day Hikes—Olympics
Hiking Glacier and Waterton Lakes National Parks
The Trail Guide to Bob Marshall Country
Hiking Arizona's Cactus Country
Hiking Zion and Bryce Canyon National Parks
Alaska on Foot: Wilderness Techniques for the Far North
Scenic Driving Alaska and the Yukon

FALCON GUIDES® Leading the Way™

All books in this popular series are regularly updated with accurate information on access, side trips, & safety.

HIKING GUIDES

Best Hikes Along the Continental Divide
Hiking Alaska
Hiking Arizona
Hiking Arizona's Cactus Country
Hiking the Beartooths
Hiking Big Bend National Park
Hiking the Bob Marshall Country
Hiking California
Hiking California's Desert Parks
Hiking Carlsbad Caverns & Guadalupe Mtns. National Parks
Hiking Colorado
Hiking Colorado, Vol. II
Hiking Colorado's Summits
Hiking Colorado's Weminuche Wilderness
Hiking the Columbia River Gorge
Hiking Florida
Hiking Georgia
Hiking Glacier/Waterton Lakes
Hiking Grand Canyon National Park
Hiking Grand Staircase-Escalante
Hiking Grand Teton National Park
Hiking Great Basin
Hiking Hot Springs in the Pacific NW
Hiking Idaho
Hiking Maine
Hiking Michigan
Hiking Minnesota
Hiking Montana
Hiking Mount Rainier National Park
Hiking Mount St. Helens
Hiking Nevada
Hiking New Hampshire
Hiking New Mexico
Hiking New York
Hiking North Carolina
Hiking North Cascades
Hiking Northern Arizona
Hiking Olympic National Park
Hiking Oregon

Hiking Oregon's Eagle Cap Wilderness
Hiking Oregon's Mt Hood/Badger Creek
Hiking Oregon's Three Sisters Country
Hiking Pennsylvania
Hiking Shenandoah National Park
Hiking the Sierra Nevada
Hiking South Carolina
Hiking South Dakota's Black Hills Cntry
Hiking Southern New England
Hiking Tennessee
Hiking Texas
Hiking Utah
Hiking Utah's Summits
Hiking Vermont
Hiking Virginia
Hiking Washington
Hiking Wyoming
Hiking Wyoming's Cloud Peak Wilderness
Hiking Wyoming's Wind River Range
Hiking Yellowstone National Park
Hiking Zion & Bryce Canyon
Exploring Canyonlands & Arches
Exploring Hawaii's Parklands

BEST EASY DAY HIKES

Beartooths
Canyonlands & Arches
Cape Cod
Colorado Springs
Glacier & Waterton Lakes
Grand Canyon
Grand Staircase-Escalante/Glen Cny
Grand Teton
Lake Tahoe
Mount Rainier
Mount St. Helens
North Cascades
Olympics
Salt Lake City
Shenandoah
Yellowstone

FALCON®

MORE THAN 5 MILLION COPIES SOLD!

FALCONGUIDES® Leading the Way™

FALCONGUIDES® are available for where-to-go hiking, mountain biking, rock climbing, walking, scenic driving, fishing, rockhounding, paddling, birding, wildlife viewing, and camping. We also have FalconGuides on essential outdoor skills and subjects and field identification. The following titles are currently available, but this list grows every year. For a free catalog with a complete list of titles, call FALCON toll-free at 1-800-582-2665.

Mountain Biking

Mountain Biking Arizona
Mountain Biking Colorado
Mountain Biking Georgia
Mountain Biking New Mexico
Mountain Biking New York
Mountain Biking Northern
   New England
Mountain Biking Oregon
Mountain Biking South Carolina
Mountain Biking Southern California
Mountain Biking Southern
   New England
Mountain Biking Utah
Mountain Biking Wisconsin
Mountain Biking Wyoming

Local Cycling Series

Fat Trax Bozeman
Mountain Biking Bend
Mountain Biking Boise
Mountain Biking Chequamegon
Mountain Biking Chico
Mountain Biking Colorado Springs
Mountain Biking Denver/Boulder
Mountain Biking Durango
Mountain Biking Flagstaff and
   Sedona
Mountain Biking Helena
Mountain Biking Moab
Mountain Biking White Mountains
Mountain Biking Utah's St. George/
   Cedar City Area

■ *To order any of these books, check with your local bookseller or call FALCON® at*
1-800-582-2665.
www.FalconOutdoors.com

FALCON®

get FALCON GUIDED

MOUNTAIN BIKING GUIDES

Mountain Biking Arizona
Mountain Biking Colorado
Mountain Biking Georgia
Mountain Biking New Mexico
Mountain Biking New York
Mountain Biking N. New England
Mountain Biking Oregon
Mountain Biking South Carolina
Mountain Biking S. New England
Mountain Biking Utah
Mountain Biking Wisconsin

LOCAL CYCLING SERIES

Bend
Boise
Bozeman
Chequamegon
Colorado Springs
Denver/Boulder
Durango
Helena
Moab
White Mountains (West)

BIRDING GUIDES

Birding Minnesota
Birding Montana
Birding Texas
Birding Utah

PADDLING GUIDES

Floater's Guide to Colorado
Paddling Montana
Paddling Okeefenokee
Paddling Oregon
Paddling Yellowstone/Grand Teton

ROCKHOUNDING GUIDES

Rockhounding Arizona
Rockhound's Guide to California
Rockhound's Guide to Colorado
Rockhounding Montana
Rockhounding Nevada
Rockhound's Guide to New Mexico
Rockhounding Texas
Rockhounding Utah
Rockhounding Wyoming

FISHING GUIDES

Fishing Alaska
Fishing Beartooths
Fishing Florida
Fishing Glacier
Fishing Maine
Fishing Montana
Fishing Wyoming
Fishing Yellowstone

To order check with you local bookseller or
call FALCON® at **1-800-582-2665**.

www.falconguide.com

FALCON®